Action Toys

Heather Amery

Illustrated by Neil Ross
Designed by David Armitage and Patricia Lee

Contributors: Andrew Calder, Diane Dorgan
Educational Adviser: Frank Blackwell

Contents

About Action Toys

This book is about lots of toys, machines, models and games to make and work. For most of them, all you need are paper, card, plastic bottles, pots and straws. You can probably find most of them at home. The measurements we have given are only a guide. You can make the things any size you like.

When you make the models and toys, you can cover them with coloured paper as you go along, or paint them when finished.
Remember to use quick-drying strong glue or gum, except for sticking expanded polystyrene tiles. For them you need a rubber-solution glue.

First Published in 1975
Usborne Publishing Ltd
Usborne House, 83-85 Saffron Hill
London EC1N 8RT

©Usborne Publishing Ltd 1989, 1975

This edition published in 1997 by Tiger Books International PLC, Twickenham

ISBN 1-85501-881-0

Printed in Italy.

Creeping Moon Bug

Wind up the motor on this Moon Bug. Put the Bug down and watch it creep along very slowly.

You will need
an empty cotton reel
a used matchstick
a strong rubber band
a candle
a stick, about 10 cm long
a sheet of thick paper
thick cardboard
corrugated cardboard
thin, bendy wire
a table knife
a pencil and scissors

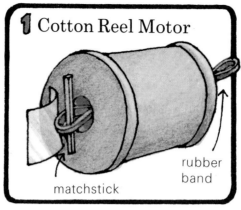

1 Cotton Reel Motor

matchstick · rubber band

Push the rubber band through the cotton reel. Push a short bit of matchstick through the loop at one end. Stick the matchstick down with a bit of tape.

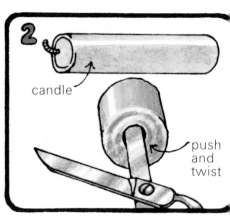

candle · push and twist

Slice a ring, about 1 cm wide, off the end of a candle with a table knife. Make a hole through it with one blade of the scissors.

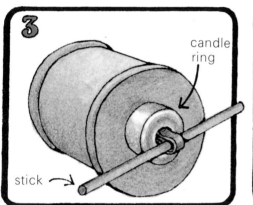

candle ring · stick

Push the free end of the rubber band through the candle ring. Then put the stick through the loop.

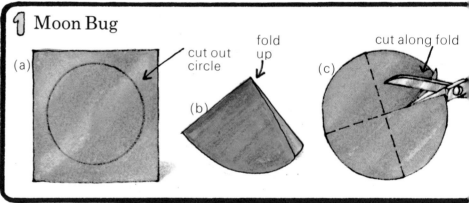

1 Moon Bug

(a) cut out circle · (b) fold up · (c) cut along fold

Draw a circle on thick paper (a). Cut it out. Fold the circle in half and then in half again (b). Unfold the paper and cut along one crease to the middle (c).

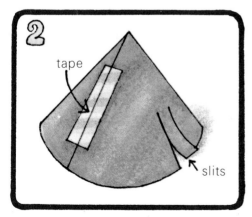

tape · slits

Curl the paper round to make a cone. Stick the edges together with tape. Cut two slits in the cone to make a flap.

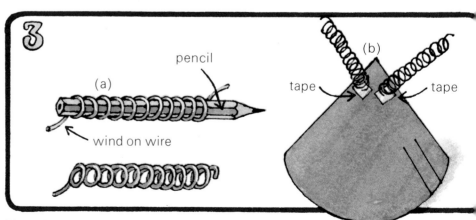

pencil · (a) wind on wire · (b) tape · tape

To make the antennae, wind a piece of bendy wire round a pencil (a). Slide it off. Curl up a second piece and stick them on the paper cone with tape (b).

Wind up the cotton reel motor. Put the cone of the Moon Bug over it, with one end of the stick poking out through the flap.

1 Climbing Bug

draw round

cardboard

Put a cotton reel down on a piece of thick cardboard. Draw round it. Draw a second circle.

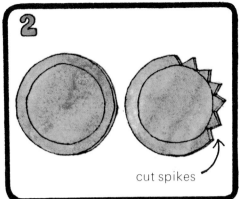

2

cut spikes

Cut out the two circles a bit bigger than the drawn lines. Cut out little bits all round both circles, like this.

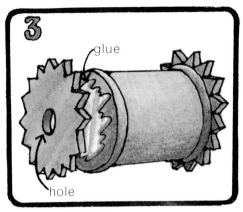

3

glue

hole

Glue a circle to each end of the cotton reel. Leave it to dry before making it into a Moon Bug.

4

Cut a long strip of corrugated cardboard about 5 cm wide. Make it into a steep road by putting things under it. Put the Bug at the bottom and let it climb.

Winding Up

wind round

Wind up the cotton reel by turning the stick round and round lots of times. Put the reel down. Put the cone over it with one end of the stick poking through the flap.

3

Rollers and Rockers

Jumping Bean

Make this Jumping Bean and stand it at the top of a gentle slope. Let it go and watch it jump and roll.

You will need
a ping pong ball
a piece of thick paper, about
    10 cm long and 5 cm wide
a marble
scissors
sticky tape

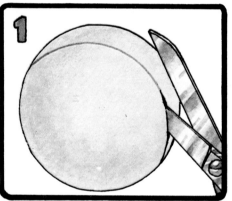

1 Push one blade of the scissors into the ping pong ball on the join line. Cut all the way round on the line.

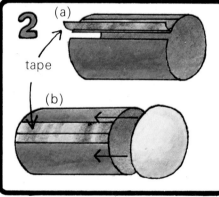

2 Roll the paper into a tube to fit just inside one half of the ping pong ball. Stick the tube with tape (a). Stick the tube to one half of the ball with tape (b).

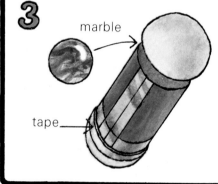

3 Put the marble in the tube. Stick the other half of the ball on the end of the tube with tape.

Rocking Egghead

Knock and push this Egghead in any way you like but he will always stand upright again.

You will need
a clean, dry eggshell with the
    top taken off
a lump of plasticine
a sheet of paper
a pencil
glue
paints
scissors

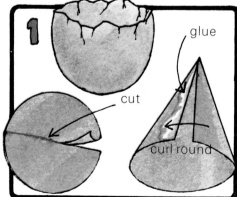

1 Draw a circle on a piece of paper, using a saucer as a guide. Cut out the circle and fold it in half. Cut along the fold. Roll one half into a cone and glue the edges.

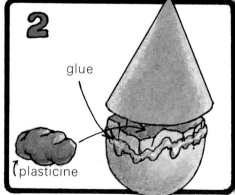

2 Stick a lump of plasticine in the bottom of the eggshell. Glue the cone to the top of the shell. Paint a funny face on it.

Floppy Hound Dog

Push the rubber bands hard to make the Dog flop about.

You will need

a strong plastic carton
2 strong rubber bands
a piece of kitchen foil rolled
 into a small ball
a drinking straw
6 pieces of very strong thread,
 each about 20 cm long
a big needle
a piece of thin cardboard,
 about 4 cm long and 4 cm wide
4 small buttons
sticky tape and scissors

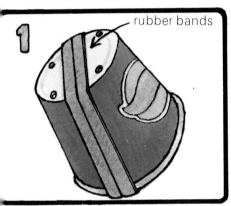

1

Put two rubber bands round the plastic carton. Poke four holes in the bottom of the carton, near the edges, with a needle.

2

straw (a)
tape
(b)
cardboard

Roll the straw tightly in sticky tape (a). Cut it into 12 pieces, all the same length. Roll up the piece of cardboard into a tube. Stick it with tape (b).

3

button
foil
straws
button

Knot two threads together. Thread the ends through a small button, the foil ball, two straw bits, another small button, and then the cardboard tube, like this.

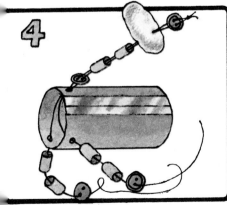

4

Pull one thread out of the needle eye. Push the other one through the other side of the tube, two straws and a button. Do the same with the other thread.

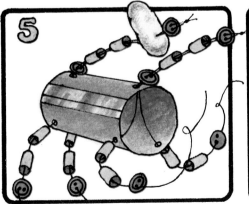

5

With two more threads, do the same at the other end of the tube to make the tail and the back legs, like this.

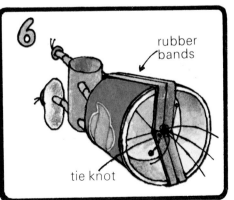

6

rubber bands
tie knot

Push a thread through each hole in the bottom of the carton. Pull two threads down on each side of the rubber bands. Tie all the threads together very tightly.

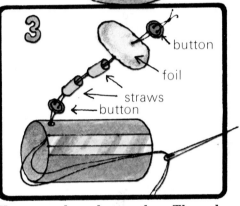

Noisy Toys

Twirling Tweeter

Hold the end of the string and twirl the Tweeter round and round your head.

You will need

a very small plastic pot or tube
  with a lid
a piece of string, about 1 metre
  long
a used matchstick
sticky tape and scissors

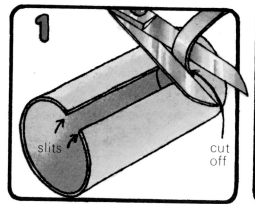

Take the lid off the plastic pot or tube. Cut two slits down one side, about $\frac{1}{2}$ cm apart. Bend back the flap and cut it off.

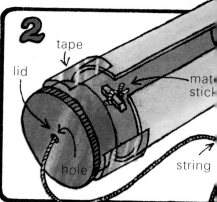

Make a hole in the lid. Push one end of a piece of string through and tie it round a matchstick. Put the lid on the pot and stick it down with tape.

Wailing Whirler

Hold the stick and swing the Whirler round and round it. Make sure the string is on the rosin. The faster the Whirler goes, the louder it will wail.

You will need

a thin stick or a pencil
a piece of nylon string or
  fishing line, about 30 cm long
a lump of rosin
  (this is sold in music shops)
a plastic carton or yoghurt pot
a used matchstick
glue and scissors

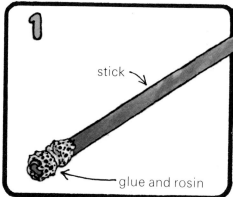

Break a small piece of rosin into bits by banging it with the handle of the scissors. Put glue on one end of the stick and dip it in the bits of rosin. Leave to dry.

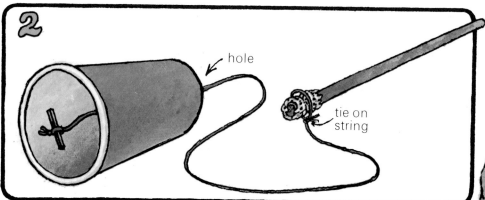

Make a hole in the bottom of a plastic carton. Push one end of the string through and tie a matchstick to the end, like this.

Loop the other end of the string loosely round the rosin on the end of the stick. Tie a knot.

Hanger Clanger

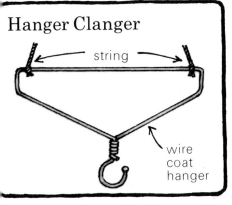

Tie the two pieces of string to a wire coat hanger, like this. Hold the other ends of the string in your ears. Bang the hanger against something and listen.

Roaring Ruler

Thread a piece of string through the hole in the end of a ruler or a thin, flat piece of wood. Tie a knot. Spin the ruler round your head to make a roaring noise.

Singing Bottle

Dip a cork in water and rub it on the side of a glass bottle. Try rubbing it gently and then hard to make bird singing noises.

Clucking Hen

Hold the carton in one hand. Hold the string very tightly between your fingers and thumb of the other hand and jerk them down the string.

You will need
2 plastic cartons or yoghurt pots
a piece of string, about 20 cm
   long
a used matchstick
a lump of rosin
quick-drying glue
scissors

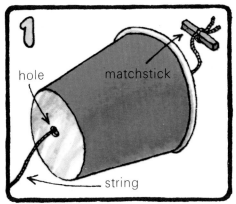

Make a hole in the bottom of a plastic carton. Push a piece of nylon thread through the hole. Tie it round a matchstick.

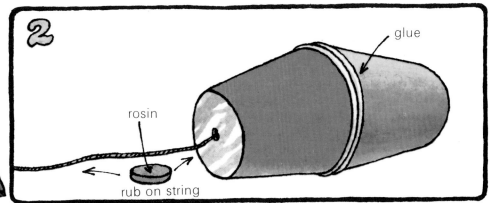

Glue a second carton to the first one, like this. Rub the string up and down on a piece of rosin.

When you have used the clucker a few times, rub on more rosin. Try making cluckers with smaller or larger plastic cartons to make different clucking noises.

Titan Traction Engine

You will need

a strong cardboard box, about 27
   cm long, 9 cm wide, 9 cm deep
thick cardboard
corrugated cardboard
2 small boxes, each about 12 cm
   long and 4 cm wide
a small, open cardboard box
5 cotton reels and 3 pencils
a cardboard tube, about 10 cm
   long
6 thin sticks or garden canes
a small polystyrene tray
1 egg holder cut from an egg box
sandpaper
scissors, glue, sticky tape,
   string, a saucer, a yoghurt pot

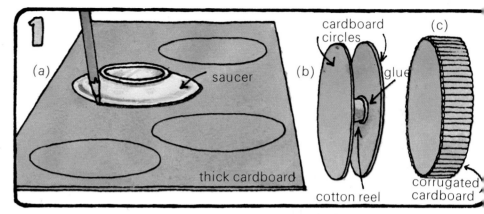

1 Draw four circles on cardboard,
using a saucer as a guide (a). Cut
them out. Glue one circle to each
end of a cotton reel (b). Glue the
other two circles to a second reel.

Glue a strip of corrugated cardboard
round the edges of two of the
cardboard circles, like this (c).
Do the same to the other two
cardboard circles.

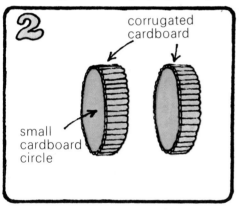

2 Make the front wheels in the same
way as the back ones, but much
smaller. The cardboard circles
should be about the same size as
the top of a small yoghurt pot.

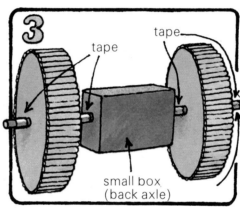

3 Push a thin stick, about 28 cm long,
through the middle of a small box.
Push one back wheel on to each end
of the stick. Wrap sticky tape round
the stick each side of both wheels.

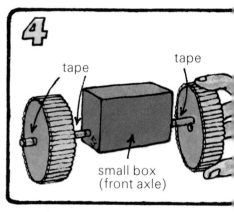

4 Push another stick through another
small box, about 1 cm from the base.
Push one front wheel on to each end
of the stick. Wrap sticky tape round
the stick each side of the wheels.

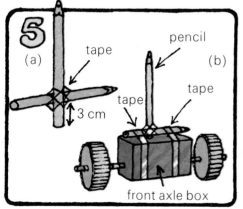

5 Tape two pencils together (a). Push
the upright pencil into the front
axle box, like this. Tape the other
pencil firmly to the axle box (b).

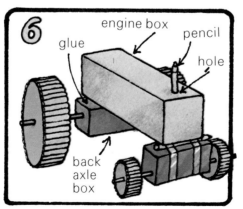

6 Glue the back axle box underneath
one end of a strong cardboard box.
Push the upright pencil on the
front axle box through a hole at
the other end of the box.

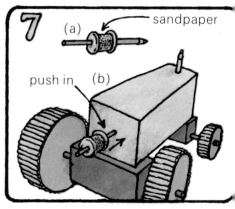

7 Glue corrugated cardboard or
sandpaper round the middle of a
cotton reel. Push a pencil through
the reel (a). Push the pencil point
into the back of the engine box (b).

Push this traction engine along and steer it by turning the cotton reel wheel.

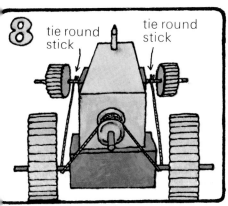

8 tie round stick   tie round stick

Wrap a piece of string round the reel, like this. Tie one end to one side of the front axle. Pull the other end tightly and tie it to the other side of the axle.

9 thin sticks

tape

Glue the open box to the back axle box, like this. Tape two sticks, about 26 cm long, to two corners. Push two sticks, about 15 cm long, into the engine box, as shown.

10 tray   egg holder

tube

glue

Put a polystyrene tray on top of the four sticks, like this. Glue a cardboard tube over the pencil at the front of the engine box. Put the egg holder on top of it.

Delta-Wing Jet

You will need

an expanded polystyrene ceiling
   tile, 30 cm square
glue for sticking material, such
   as Copydex
a small lump of plasticine
a strip of cardboard, about
   10 cm long and 5 cm wide
3 long, big-headed pins
a big sheet of paper
a strong rubber band
a long cardboard box
a ruler and a ball-point pen
scissors and paints

Launch your jet and see how far and
how fast you can make it fly. Or
make two jets and have indoor or
outdoor races.

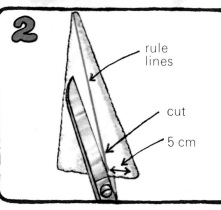

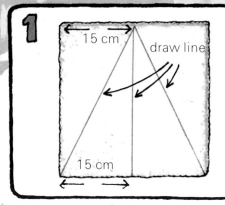

1 draw line

15 cm

15 cm

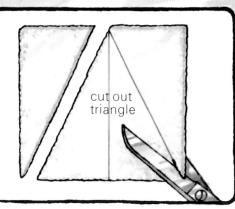

cut out
triangle

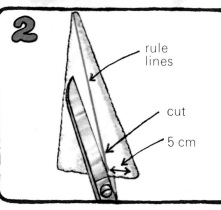

2 rule
lines

cut

5 cm

Measure 15 cm along the top and
bottom of the tile and make marks.
Draw a line between the two marks.
Draw lines from the top mark to the
two bottom corners (a).

Carefully cut along the two lines
from the top to the corners with
scissors (b). Be careful not to break
the cut-off pieces.

Measure 5 cm along the short edge of
one cut-off piece. Draw a line from the
mark to the point. Cut along the drawn
line. Throw away the small cut-off
piece.

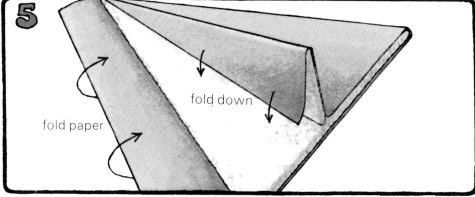

5 fold paper

fold down

6 pin
glue on
cardboard

Put the jet down on a large sheet of
paper. Fold the paper round the
wings very neatly. Press it up the
fin and glue the edges of the paper
together.

Trim the edges of the paper on the
fin. When the glue is dry, paint the
paper in different colours.

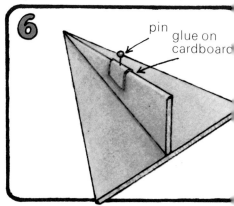

Fold the strip of cardboard in half.
Glue it to the fin, about half-way
along. Push a big-headed pin into
the middle of the cardboard strip,
like this.

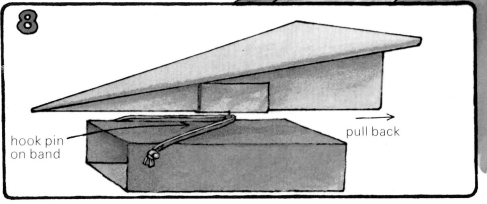

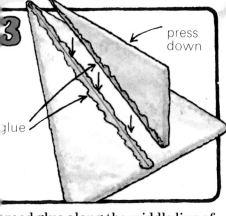

3

press down

glue

read glue along the middle line of e big triangle and along one edge the cut-off piece. Leave it to dry. en press the cut-off piece to the iangle, like this.

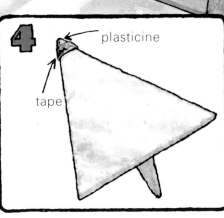

4

plasticine

tape

Turn the jet over. Flatten a small lump of plasticine. Stick it to the nose of the jet with tape.

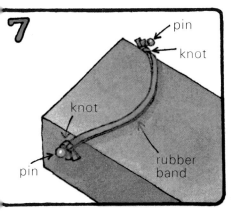

7

pin

knot

knot

pin

rubber band

o make the launcher, cut a rubber and in half. Push a big-headed pin nd to each side of a long cardboard ox. Tie the ends of the band to the ig-headed pins.

8

hook pin on band

pull back

To launch the jet, hook the pin on the jet fin on to the band on the launcher. Hold the jet fin and pull it gently backwards.

Slide the jet back along the box. Tilt the box slightly upwards. Point the jet and let it go.

Dizzy, the Dashing Dragon

Pull up the curtain ring on the Dragon's head and let it go to make him rush along.

You will need

a piece of cardboard, about 12 cm long and 12 cm wide
a lump of modelling clay
a rubber band
a plastic drinking straw
a piece of nylon thread or very thin string, about 70 cm long
a small curtain ring
a big hairpin
a piece of thin paper, about 12 cm wide and 60 cm long
sticky tape and glue
scissors

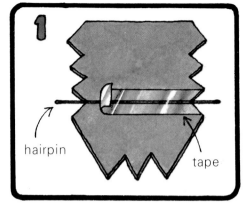

Cut a head shape out of cardboard, like this. Straighten a hairpin. Stick the pin with tape across the head, quite close to one end.

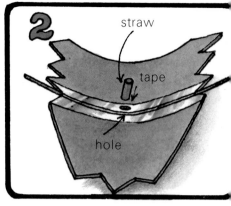

Make a hole in the middle of the head, just behind the hairpin. Push a short piece of straw into the hole. Glue it in place. Bend the head into curved shape.

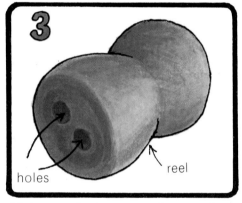

Make a reel, about 4 cm long and 3 cm across, out of modelling clay in this shape. Make two holes right through it, like this.

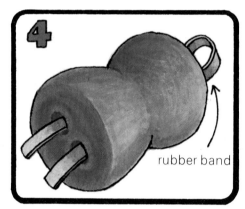

Cut a rubber band. Push the ends through the two holes in the clay reel, like this. Leave the reel until it is dry.

Knot the ends of the rubber band. Tie one end of the nylon thread on the reel. Wind all the thread on to the reel. Push the free end through the straw.

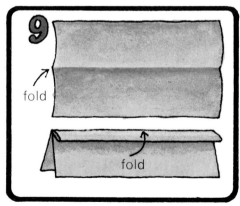

To make the dragon's body, fold the long piece of paper in half (a). Fold over the folded edge to make a flap about 1 cm wide (b).

Open out the paper. Make folds, about 2 cm wide, all along it, like this. Turn the paper over and crease all the folds the other way.

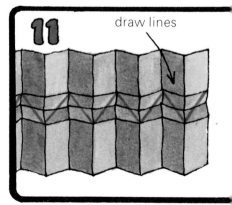

Open the paper again. Draw zig-zag lines from the top fold line to the bottom fold line, like this.

12

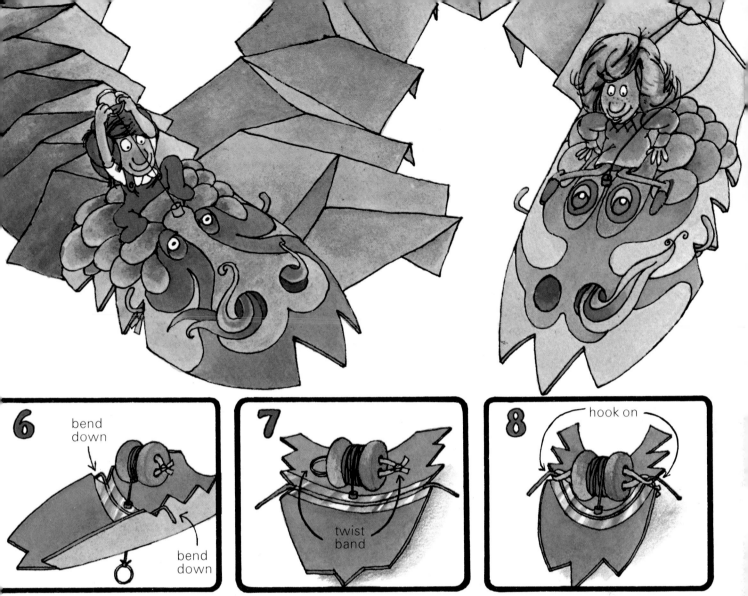

6 bend down

bend down

e one end of the thread to a curtain
ng on top of the head. Bend the
nds of the hairpin down.

7 twist band

Turn the reel round and round to
wind the thread very tight. Give one
twist to each end of the rubber band.

8 hook on

Hook each end of the rubber band on
to the ends of the hairpin. Bend the
head again to make sure the reel
will not rub on it.

12

old the paper along all the drawn
nes. Pinch together all the drawn
nes and pleat the paper with your
ngers, like this.

13 tape

Stick one end of the paper body to
the edge of the cardboard head, like
this. Paint the dragon's head with
lots of different colours.

To make a longer tail, fold up a
second strip of thin paper in the
same way as the first one. Glue it
to the end of the first strip.

Two-Stage Saturn Rocket

You will need
a long cardboard tube
2 short cardboard tubes
3 paper clips
2 rubber bands
a piece of string, about as long
    as the long tube
a piece of very thin cloth,
    about 20 cm long and 20 cm
    wide
4 pieces of cotton thread, each
    about 25 cm long
a small curtain ring
thick and thin cardboard
sticky tape and glue
scissors and a pencil

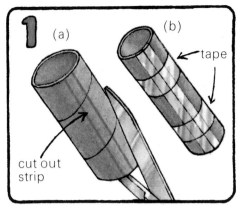

1 (a) (b) tape
cut out strip

Slide a short cardboard tube into
the long one. If it is too big, cut out
a strip (a). Hold the cut edges
together and stick them with tape
to make a smaller tube (b).

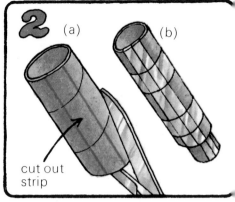

2 (a) (b)
cut out strip

Cut a wider strip out of a second
short tube (a). Stick the edges
together with tape. Slide it inside
the first tube (b).

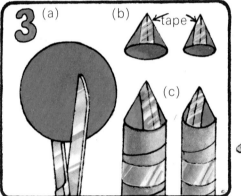

3 (a) (b) tape (c)

Cut a small circle out of thin
cardboard. Cut it in half (a). Curl
both halves into cones and stick
with tape (b). Glue one cone to the
top of each tube (c).

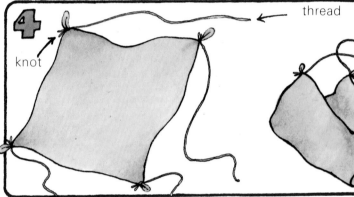

4 thread
knot
glue on thread

To make a drogue parachute, tie a
piece of cotton thread tightly to
each corner of the piece of cloth.

Glue the ends of the four pieces of
thread to the end of the small
rocket, like this. Make sure the
threads are not twisted together.

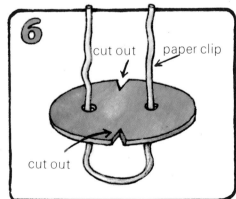

6 cut out   paper clip
cut out

Cut two little triangles out of the
edge of the cardboard circle.
Straighten a paper clip. Push the
ends through the holes in the circle,
like this.

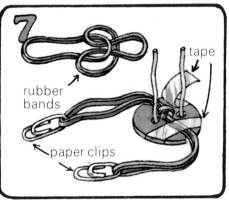

7 rubber bands   tape
paper clips

Loop two rubber bands together (a).
Put them on the circle over the
cut-out triangles (b). Stick them
down with tape. Hook a paper clip
on to the end of each band.

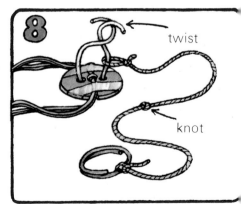

8 twist
knot

Twist the ends of the paper clip
together and bend back. Tie the
string on to the paper clip. Make a
knot in the middle. Tie the curtain
ring on the other end.

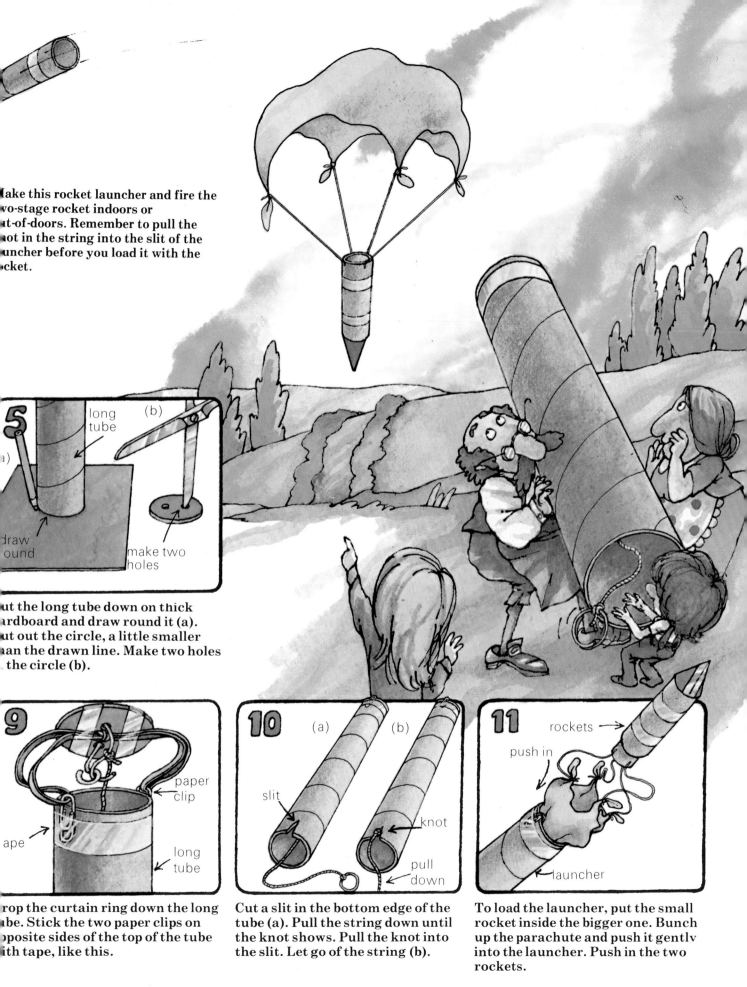

Make this rocket launcher and fire the two-stage rocket indoors or out-of-doors. Remember to pull the knot in the string into the slit of the launcher before you load it with the rocket.

5

(a)   (b)

long tube

draw round

make two holes

Put the long tube down on thick cardboard and draw round it (a). Cut out the circle, a little smaller than the drawn line. Make two holes in the circle (b).

9

paper clip

tape

long tube

Drop the curtain ring down the long tube. Stick the two paper clips on opposite sides of the top of the tube with tape, like this.

10

(a)   (b)

slit

knot

pull down

Cut a slit in the bottom edge of the tube (a). Pull the string down until the knot shows. Pull the knot into the slit. Let go of the string (b).

11

rockets

push in

launcher

To load the launcher, put the small rocket inside the bigger one. Bunch up the parachute and push it gently into the launcher. Push in the two rockets.

15

High-Wire Walker

Tie a very long piece of string across a room. Put the Walker on it. Push the plasticine to make it swing and move the Walker.

You will need
a matchbox
4 plastic drinking straws
a sheet of paper
a piece of thin cardboard
a piece of string, about 60 cm long
a long big-headed pin
plasticine
sticky tape and glue
scissors

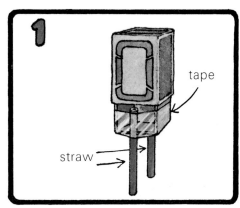

1

Cut a straw in half and then in half again. Push the tray half out of the matchbox. Stick two pieces of straw to the tray with tape to make legs. Push in the tray.

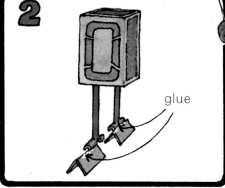

2

Cut two little slits in the end of each leg. Bend back the ends. Fold two small pieces of cardboard in half. Glue one to the end of each leg to make feet.

3

Cut a strip of cardboard about twice as long as the top of the matchbox. Fold it in half. Glue the ends to the top of the matchbox, like this.

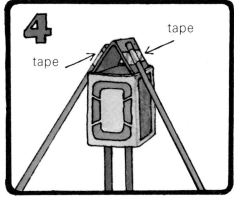

4

Stick a straw on each side of the folded cardboard with tape, like this, to make arms.

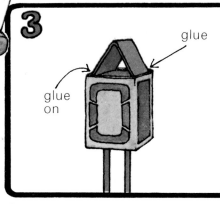

5

Roll up a thin strip of paper to make a head. Stick it with tape. Cut out a paper circle. Push the pin through it and into the head. Pin it to the top of the body.

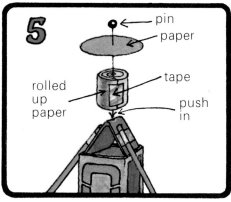

6

Cut a straw in half. Stick one half to each arm with tape. Stick the ends of the string on to the straws with tape. Put a lump of plasticine in the middle of the string.

Trick Cyclist

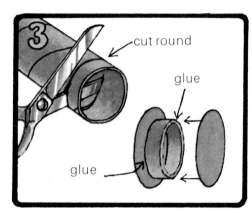

Balance the Cyclist on a very long piece of string. Tilt the string downwards to make the wheel roll round.

You will need
a piece of cardboard, about
   30 cm long and 15 cm wide
a cardboard tube
a drinking straw
a hairpin
a sheet of paper
plasticine
a pencil
glue and scissors

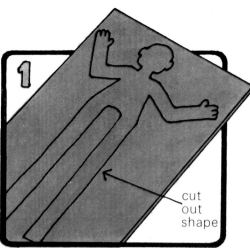

Draw a thin man, about 30 cm tall, on cardboard. Make the legs about twice as long as the body. Cut out the shape, with a wide space between the legs, like this.

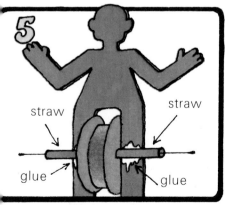

Put the end of a cardboard tube on some cardboard and draw two circles. Cut out the circles, about __ cm wider than the lines.

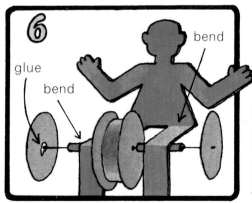

Cut a band, about 1 cm wide, off the end of the tube (a). Glue a circle on each side of the band to make a wheel (b).

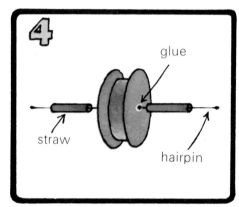

Straighten a hairpin and push it through the middle of the wheel. Glue it to the wheel. Push a short bit of straw on the hairpin on each side of the wheel.

Put the wheel between the legs of the cardboard man, with a gap at the top. Make sure the wheel turns easily. Glue the two bits of straw to the legs, like this.

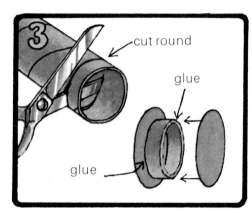

Bend the man's legs round the straw and bend him again at the top of his legs. Cut out two small paper circles. Glue one to each end of the hairpin.

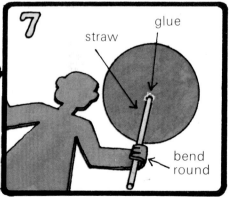

Cut out a paper circle. Glue it to the end of a bit of straw. Glue the other end to the man's hand. Glue a small lump of plasticine to the ends of the man's legs.

17

Fire-Fighting Truck

You will need
a shoe box, or an oblong
  cardboard box
a small cardboard box
4 empty cotton reels
very thin string
3 rubber bands
3 strips of thick cardboard, each
  about 30 cm long and 6 cm wide
2 paper fasteners
2 used matchsticks
3 pencils or thin sticks
a ball-point pen, without the
  ink tube, and a balloon
a plastic carton
scissors and glue

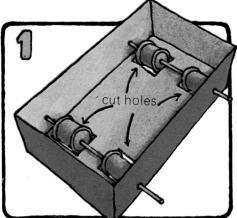

Cut four square holes in the shoe
box bottom. Make two holes in each
side. Push two pencils through one
side. Slide two cotton reels on to
each pencil and push out the sides.

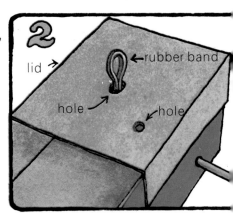

Cut the box lid in half. Make a hole
in the middle of one half. Push a
rubber band end through and slide
on a matchstick underneath. Make
a second hole. Put on the lid.

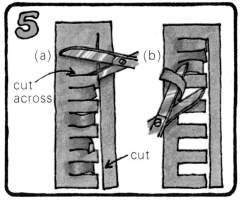

Cut up one side of the second
cardboard strip. Then cut across (a).
Cut out every other piece (b) to
make a ladder. Cut a second ladder
in the same way.

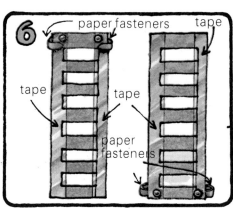

Put sticky tape down the sides of
each ladder. Push two paper
fasteners through the top of one
ladder and the bottom of the other.
Bend over the ends, like this.

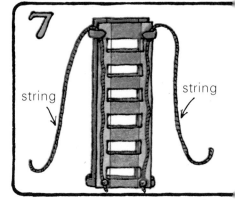

Cut two strings, each twice as long
as the ladders. Put the two ladders
together, like this. Tie a string to
each bottom fastener and loop it
over the top ones.

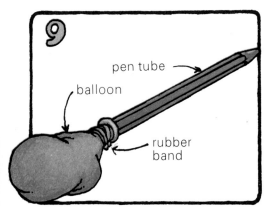

Push the pen tube into the neck of
the balloon. Wind a rubber band
round the balloon neck several
times to make it very tight.

To fill the balloon, put the pen tube
up a water tap. Turn on the tap.
When the balloon is about as big as
an orange, put the pen top on very
quickly.

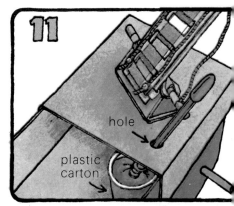

Put the balloon in a plastic carton
to catch the drips of water. Push the
pen tube through the hole in the box
lid from the inside.

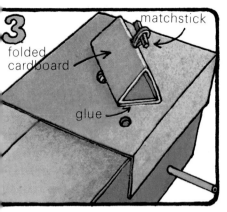

3

folded cardboard

matchstick

glue

ld a strip of cardboard up to make
riangle, like this. Make a hole in
e flat side and one fold. Push the
nd through. Slide a matchstick
rough loop of the band.

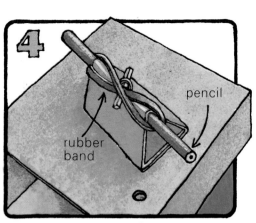

4

pencil

rubber band

Put a pencil through the cardboard
triangle. Loop a rubber band over
one end of the pencil. Twist it in the
middle and hook it over the other
end of the pencil.

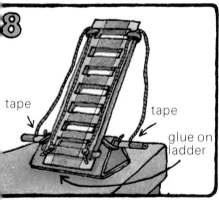

8

tape

tape

glue on ladder

ue the underneath ladder to the
angle on the box lid. Wind the
d of each string round the pencil
d stick it with tape.

Push the fire engine to a pretend
fire. Twist the pencil to wind up the
ladder and take off the pen top to
squirt the water.

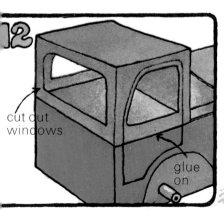

12

cut out windows

glue on

make a cab, cut out the sides of
mall box for the windscreen and
e windows. Glue the box to the
nt of the fire truck.

Power Pacer

Wind the propeller on this boat about 20 times. Put the boat in water and let it go.

You will need
a plastic squeezy bottle
a piece of plastic cut from the side of a plastic bottle
a ball-point pen, with the ink tube taken out
3 strong rubber bands
a piece of thin bendy wire, about 10 cm long
a used matchstick
kitchen foil
scissors

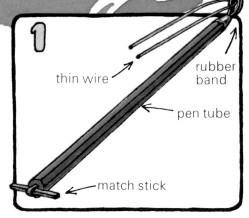

Push a rubber band through the pen tube. Push a matchstick through the loop at one end. Hook a piece of bendy wire through the other end.

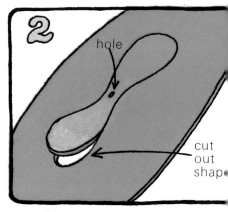

To make the propeller, draw the shape of a figure eight, about 6 cm long, on the plastic piece. Cut it out. Make a small hole in the middle.

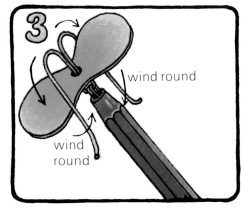

Push the ends of the wire through the hole in the propeller. Wind them tightly round, like this.

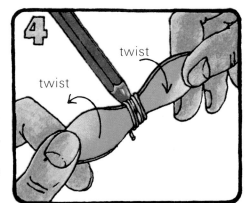

Hold the ends of the propeller like this. Twist the right side towards you and the left side away from you.

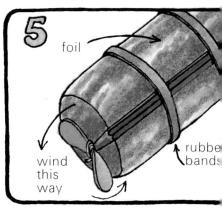

Wrap the plastic bottle tightly in foil. Put the pen tube against one side, with the propeller sticking out from the flat end. Put on two rubber bands, like this.

Balloon Record Breaker

Try making two boats and have races with them. The bigger you blow up the balloon, the faster and farther the boat will go.

You will need

plastic squeezy bottle
ball-point pen, with the
  ink tube taken out
balloon
small rubber band
plasticine
scissors

1 Push one blade of the scissors into one side of the plastic bottle. Cut out a long, wide strip, like this.

cut out

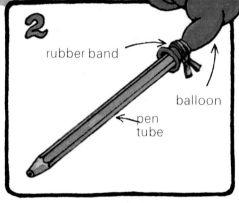

2 Push the pen tube into the neck of the balloon. Wind a rubber band very tightly round the neck of the balloon.

rubber band
balloon
pen tube

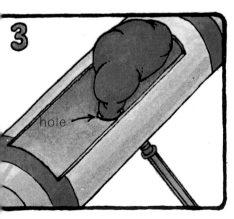

3 Make a hole in the plastic bottle on the opposite side to the cut-out side. Push the balloon through the hole from the outside.

hole

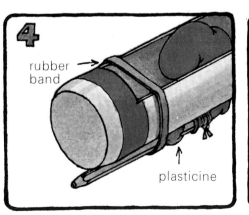

4 Bend back the pen tube towards the flat end of the bottle. Put a rubber band round it, like this, to keep it in place. Press some plasticine round the pen tube.

rubber band
plasticine

5 To make the boat go along, blow up the balloon through the pen tube. Put the boat quickly in water and let it go.

blow in here

Eager Weaver

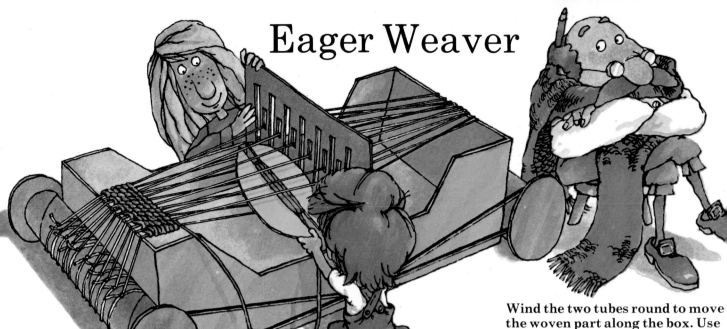

Wind the two tubes round to move the woven part along the box. Use different coloured wools on the shuttle to make woven patterns. O[r] tie different colours to the tubes.

Make this loom and use it to weave small scarves, ties and belts. Or weave long pieces and sew them together to make patchwork blankets.

You will need
a cardboard shoe box or strong cardboard box
thick cardboard
2 long cardboard tubes
4 large rubber bands
coloured wools
a pencil and a ruler
glue and sticky tape
scissors

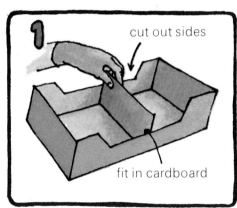

1 cut out sides / fit in cardboard

Cut out the sides of the box, like this. Cut a piece of cardboard for the handle, about 9 cm wide and as long as the width of the box. Make sure it fits the box.

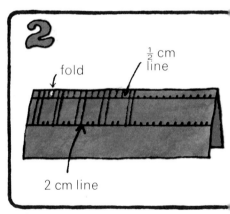

2 fold / $\frac{1}{2}$ cm line / 2 cm line

Fold the cardboard in half. Rule lines $\frac{1}{2}$ cm and 2 cm from the fold. Mark every $\frac{1}{2}$ cm along both lines. Rule long and short boxes, with a space between them, like this.

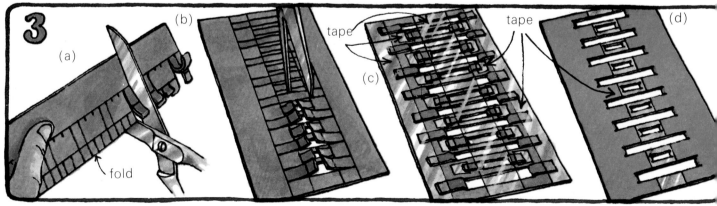

3 (a) (b) (c) (d) / tape / tape / fold

Cut along all the lines from the fold (a). Unfold the cardboard. Snip every other cut bit along the fold (b).

When all the bits have been cut, fold them back. Fold the short cuts back to the $\frac{1}{2}$ cm line and the long cuts to the 2 cm line. Stick all the flaps down with tape (c).

Stick tape along the fold on both sides of the cardboard (d). Snip out all the bits of tape in the spaces. Th[is] piece of cardboard is the heddle.

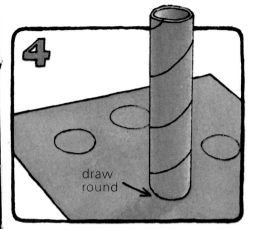

4

draw round

Using the end of a tube as a guide, draw four circles on cardboard. Cut out the circles a little larger than the lines. Glue a circle to each end of the tubes.

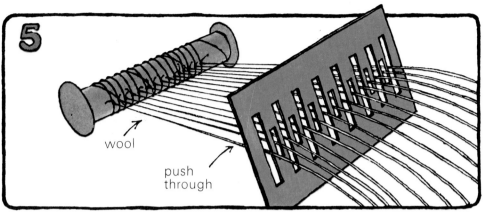

5

wool

push through

Cut 15 pieces of wool at least 50 cm long. Knot one piece round one end of a tube. Push the other end through the first hole in the end of the heddle.

Tie on another piece of wool. Push it through the second hole in the heddle. Tie on the rest of the wool, pushing it through the holes in the heddle, like this.

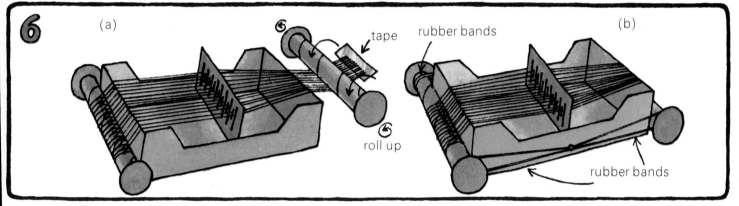

6 (a) tape rubber bands (b) roll up rubber bands

Put the heddle in the middle of the box. Put the tube with the wool on the outside at one end. Pull all the free ends of the wool over the other end of the box.

Put a second tube over the ends of the wool. Stick the ends to the tube with tape (a).

Knot two rubber bands together. Hook them over the tubes on one side of the box (b). Knot two more bands and hook them on to the other ends of the tubes.

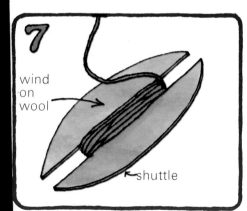

7

wind on wool

shuttle

Cut out a piece of cardboard a little longer than the width of the box. Cut it into this shape. This is the shuttle. Wind on a very long piece of wool, like this.

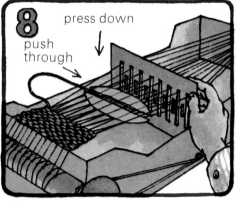

8

press down

push through

Tie the end of the wool on the shuttle to a strand of wool on the loom. Press the heddle down and push the shuttle through between the strands of wool.

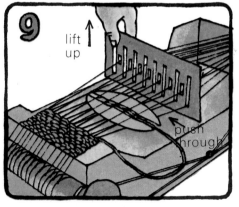

9

lift up

push through

To weave the next line, lift the heddle up. Push the shuttle through from the other side. Push the heddle against the woven part each time you weave a new line.

Mr Twitch

Turn Mr Twitch upside down to make his arms go round. When they stop, turn him up again.

You will need
2 plastic cartons or yoghurt pots
a piece of thin cardboard
4 used matchsticks
2 long needles
table salt
a drinking straw
glue and sticky tape
a needle and thread
a pencil and scissors

1

draw line

Draw four circles on thick cardboard, using the top of a plastic carton as a guide. Cut out the circles.

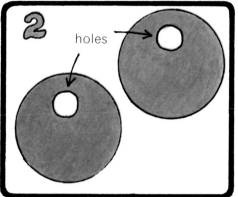

2

holes

Cut a round hole in each of the cardboard circles, near one edge, like this.

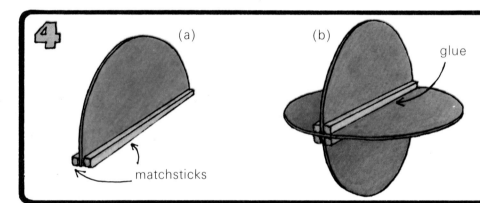

4

(a)

(b)

glue

matchsticks

Fold a third cardboard circle in half. Cut along the fold. Glue a matchstick on each side of one half-circle (a). Glue matchsticks to the other half-circle.

Glue the uncut circle to the matchsticks on one half-circle. Glue the second half-circle to the circle, like this (b).

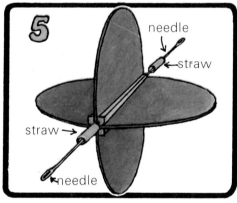

5

needle

straw

straw

needle

Push a needle into each end of the matchsticks. Slide a very short bit of straw on to the end of each needle.

7

(a)

slit

cut slit

hole

(b)

push down slit

push down slit

Stand the tube on end and cut two slits about half-way down it on both sides (a). Make a small hole at the end of each slit.

Push the cardboard circles down inside the tube with the needles in the slits (b). Spin the circles to make sure they turn easily. If not, trim a bit off the circles.

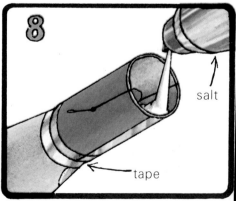

8

salt

tape

Pour some table salt into the tube. Put in enough to almost fill the plastic carton.

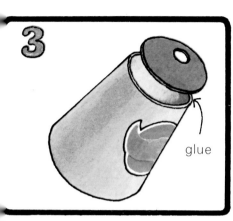

3

Glue one cardboard circle to the top of each of the plastic cartons. Use lots of glue to stick them very firmly.

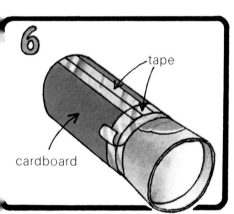

6

tape

cardboard

Roll a piece of thin cardboard very tightly round the top of a plastic carton. Stick it with tape to make a tube. Tape the tube very firmly to the carton.

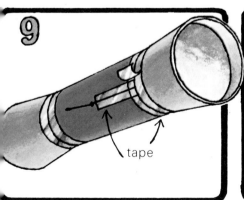

9

tape

Push the top of the second plastic carton into the top of the tube. Wrap sticky tape very tightly round the end of the tube to stick it to the carton.

10

thread

knot

Cut the shape of two long arms out of thin paper. Cut them at the elbows. Cut out fingers and thumbs. Use a needle and thread to join the arms and fingers, like this.

11

glue

glue

Push the top of each arm on to the ends of the needles in the cardboard tube. Put one arm up and the other down. Glue them to the needles.

Formula XF Bullet

You will need
a sheet of paper, 29 cm long
    and 21 cm wide
2 ball-point pens without
    the ink tubes
a ball-point pen top
2 plastic drinking straws or
    very thin sticks
a bead
bendy wire and a paper clip
a matchbox cover
thick cardboard
stiff plastic cut from a
    plastic bottle
a strong rubber band
glue and sticky tape
a pencil and scissors

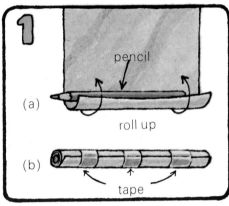

1 Put the pencil on one edge of the paper. Roll the paper very tightly round the pencil (a). Stick the end of the rolled paper with tape (b). Shake out the pencil.

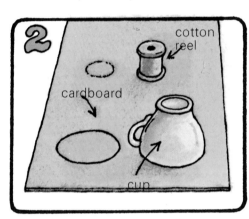

2 Cut two small circles out of cardboard, for the front wheels. Use a cotton reel as a guide. Cut out two big circles for the back wheels. Use a cup as a guide.

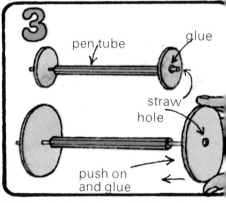

3 Make a hole in the middle of each wheel. Push a straw through a pen tube. Push a small wheel on each end and glue them on. Do the same with the back wheels.

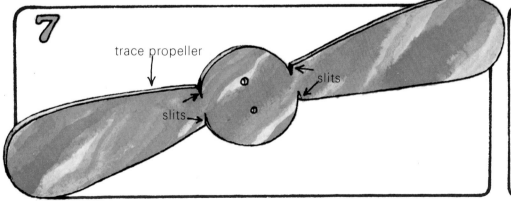

7 Trace this propeller shape on thin or see-through paper. Cut out the shape. Hold it down on a piece of plastic. Draw round the shape.

Cut the shape out very carefully. Cut two little slits on each side of the round part. Make two holes in the round middle part.

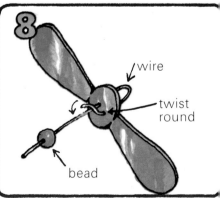

8 Loop a piece of bendy wire through the holes in the propeller. Twist one end round the other end, like this. Push the long end through a bead and pull it tight.

26

4
tape • tape • paper tube

...ut the paper tube across the two
...n tubes, like this. Wind sticky
...pe round the paper tube and each
...n tube to fix them in place.

5
matchbox cover • tape • tape • big wheel

Cut one side off a matchbox cover.
Put it, cut side down, on the paper
tube at the end with the big wheels.
Tilt it forward a little, like this,
and stick it to the tube with tape.

6
cut off tip • tape

Cut the end of a pen top with
scissors. Put it on top of the
matchbox cover, like this. Stick
it down very firmly with tape.

9
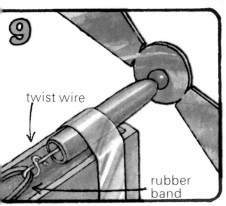
twist wire • rubber band

...ush the long end of the wire
...hrough the pen top on the car.
...oop a rubber band on to the wire
...nd twist the wire round, like this.

10
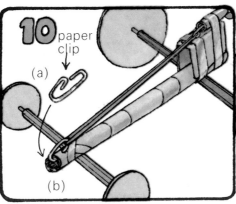
paper clip • (a) • (b)

Bend open a paper clip (a). Push one
loop into the end of the paper tube.
Hook the end of the rubber band
on to the other loop of the paper
clip (b).

11
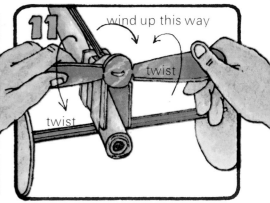
wind up this way • twist • twist

Hold the propeller like this. Twist
the right side towards the front of
the car. Twist the left side the other
way. Wind up the propeller this way
about 20 times.

Water Clock

Make this water clock and use it to tell the time. If the hand goes round too fast, drop a drawing pin or big-headed pin into the bottom of the plastic bottle. Or push a thin piece of stick into the hole. If the cork does not go down with the water, put a bit more plasticine on the string. Remember to empty the pot or bowl in the bottom of the box when it is full of water.

You will need

a plastic squeezy bottle
a large, strong cardboard box, about 40 cm high
2 knitting needles
2 corks
4 pieces of string, each about as long as the width of the box
a sheet of paper
a piece of cardboard
plasticine
a pot or bowl
a pencil
scissors and glue

Cut the bottom off a plastic bottle. Make four holes in it, near the bottom edge (a).

Push a piece of string through each hole. Tie a knot on the end of each string on the outside of the bottle (b).

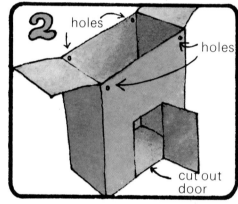

Open the top of the box. Cut a door in one side, near the bottom. Make a hole in each corner near the top of the box.

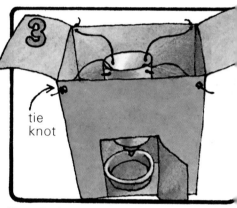

Put the bottle inside the box. Push one string through each hole in the top of the box and tie a knot on the end. Put a pot or bowl in the bottom of the box.

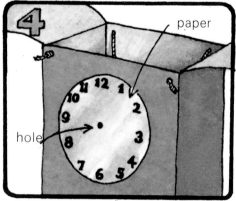

Cut out a paper circle. Write on it the numbers 1 to 12, like the face of a clock. Stick it to the front of the box, near the top. Make a hole in the middle of the circle.

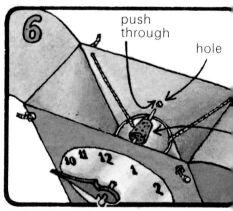

Cut a clock hand from a piece of cardboard. Make a hole in the round end (a). Push a knitting needle through the hole and glue the hand to the end (b).

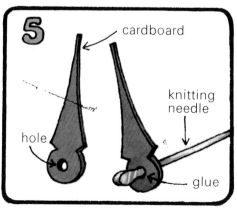

Make a hole through a cork with scissors. Push the knitting needle through the clock face. Push the cork on to the needle and push the needle out the back of the box.

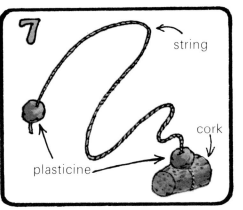

Cut a string a little longer than the height of the box. Tie a cork on one end. Put some plasticine on the string near the cork. Put another lump on the other end.

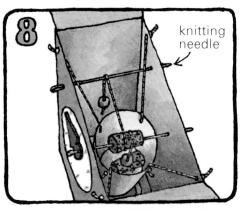

Put the string round the cork, like this. Drop the cork end into the bottle. Push a second knitting needle through the box near the first one. Loop the string over it.

Pour some water into the plastic bottle. Pull up the plasticine end of the string so that the cork just rests on the water.

Grand Prix Car Races

Make this track and race your toy cars all round the floor. It will work best on a floor without a carpet. You can make the circuits any shape you like by putting the strings round more chair legs. If the strings slip on the wheels, push the chairs away from the wheels to make them tight again.

Before a race, decide how many times the cars should go round the tracks. It could be twice for a short race or ten times for a long one. The winner is the first car to reach the finishing line.

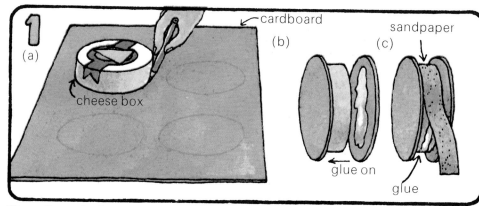

You will need
2 small, toy cars
a round, cardboard cheese box
2 pieces of thick string, each
    about 5 metres long
2 horseshoe magnets
a sheet of sandpaper
2 big nails
2 pencils
2 ball-point pen tops
cardboard
4 empty tins
strong glue

1 (a) cheese box — cardboard (b) sandpaper (c) glue on glue

Draw four circles on cardboard, using the cheese box as a guide (a). Cut out the four circles, making them about 1 cm bigger than the drawn lines.

Glue two circles on each side of the cheese box lid and bottom to make two wheels (b). Glue a strip of sandpaper round the wheels (c).

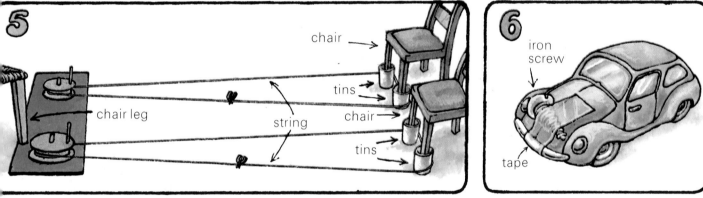

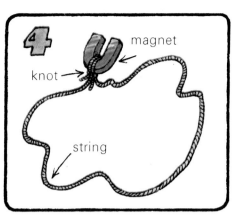

Push two nails through each end of a large sheet of cardboard. Stick a piece of tape over each nail head. Push a nail through the middle of each wheel, like this.

Glue a ball-point pen top over each nail. Make sure no glue goes on the nails. Push a pencil through each wheel near the edge. Glue them in place.

Tie the ends of each piece of string together. Tie a magnet to the knot in each piece of string.

Put the cardboard with the wheels down on the floor. Put a table or chair leg on it. Loop one string round each wheel. Put the front legs of two chairs in tins.

Put two chair legs over each string, like this. Push the chairs gently away from the wheels until the strings are stretched tight.

Try sticking the cars to the magnets. If they will not stick, put a small, fat, iron screw or bit of iron on the front of each car. Stick it firmly in place with tape.

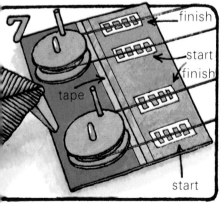

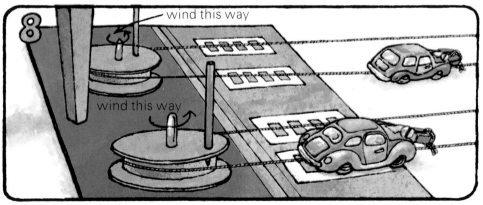

Stick a second piece of cardboard in front of the first one with tape. Draw or paint a starting and finishing line under each string.

To race the cars, wind the magnets back to the starting lines. Stick a car to each magnet. When someone says 'go', two players each wind a handle to move the cars forward.

If a car comes off a magnet, wind the handle the other way to move the magnet back again to the car. Or go to the car and stick it on the magnet again.

Snow Storm

Make a mountain with little houses, or a hill, and stick on little plastic animals and people. Shake the jar to start the snow storm and watch it slowly settle.

You will need
a short glass jar with a
   screw-on lid
different coloured plasticine
waterproof inks
waterproof glue
french chalk (this is sold in
   chemist shops)
cold, boiled water

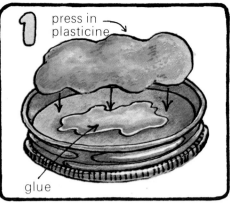

press in plasticine

glue

Take the lid off the jar. Spread glue on the inside. Press some plasticine on the glue, keeping it away from the edge of the lid.

Press on more plasticine to make a high mountain. Shape small blocks for houses. Draw in doors and windows with waterproof ink. Press them to the mountain.

french chalk

cold boiled water

Pour cold, boiled water into the jar, almost to the top. Put in one heaped teaspoon of french chalk. Stir it until all the lumps have been mixed in.

screw on lid

When the glue on the lid is dry, turn the lid over. Screw it on to the jar very tightly. Some of the water may run over.

Try making different scenes in other glass jars with lots of coloured plasticine.

You could make a Christmas scene and put gold and silver glitter bits in the water.